DAY TRADING STOCKS

The Blueprint to Stock Market Investing and Trading for Financial Freedom

Written By Michael Stevenson

Edition 2019

© Copyright 2019 by – All rights reserved

This document is geared towards providing exact and reliable information in regards to the topic and issue covered. The publication is sold with the idea that the publisher is not required to render accounting, officially permitted, or otherwise, qualified services. If advice is necessary legal or professional, a practiced individual in the profession should be ordered.

From a Declaration of Principles which was accepted and approved equally by a Committee of the American Bar Association and a Committee of Publishers and Associations.

In no way is it legal to reproduce, duplicate or transmit any part of this document in either electronic means or in oriented format. Recording of this publication is strictly prohibited and any storage of this document is not allowed unless with written permission from the publisher. All rights reserved.

The information provided herein is stated to be truthful and consistent, in that any liability, in terms of inattention or otherwise, by any usage or abuse of any policies, processes, or directions contained within is the solitary and utter responsibility of the recipient reader. Under no circumstances will any legal responsibility or blame be held against the publisher for any reparation, damages, or monetary loss due to the information herein, either directly or indirectly.

Respective authors own all copyrights not held by the publisher.

The information herein is offered for informational purposes solely, and is universal as so. The presentation of the information is without contract or any type of guarantee assurance.

The trademarks that are used are without any consent and the publication of the trademark is without permission or backing by the trademark owner. All trademarks and brands within this book are for clarifying purposes and are the owned by the owners themselves, not affiliated to with this document.

Disclaimer

The content of this eBook has been checked and compiled with great care. For the completeness, correctness and topicality of the contents however no guarantee or guarantee can be taken over. The content of this eBook represents the personal experience and opinion of the author and is for entertainment purposes only. The content should not be confused with medical help. There will be no legal

Responsibility or liability for damages resulting from counterproductive exercise or errors by the reader. No guarantee can be given for success. The author therefore assumes no responsibility for the non-achievement of the goals described in the book.

Table of Contents

Day Trading - The Dream Of Quick Money 1

Fundamentals And Strategy Development Of Day Trading 11

Online Trading - Fast Money Or Hard Work? 27

The Successful Traders 38

The 10 Golden Tips That Every Trader Should Know 44

Stock Market: Definition, Characteristics, And Importance 48

The 7 Best Investment Books For Beginners 61

6 Myths About The Stock Market That Can Ruin You 70

The Stock Trading Software 2019 - The Best Providers And Their Software In Comparison 74

Warren Buffett: The Most Successful Investor In The 20th Century 81

10 Precautions To Take Before Investing In A Stock Market 87

Key Questions To Learn To Invest In The Stock Market 92

Which Method Is Better To Make Money In The Stock Market? 96

How To Achieve Consistency In Trading? Main Basic Rules To Follow 100

5 Financial Tools Essential For Traders And Investors .. 105

Conclusion: Make Trading Worth Your Time 114

Appreciation 116

DAY TRADING - THE DREAM OF QUICK MONEY

Day trading is the supreme discipline of active trading and, if implemented appropriately, offers attractive profits. But which markets are suitable for day trading? Which strategies promise success and why do the less successful daytraders fail? How much capital is required and how much profit is realistic? These and other questions are answered in this great ebook we have thoroughly prepared for you.

Definition

Day trading basically refers to the same day trading on the financial markets: in the narrower definition, all positions are opened and closed within one day. In practice, the distinction from relatively short-term trading strategies with a time horizon of a few days to several weeks is not always that easy.

In terms of taxation, day trading does not differ significantly from approaches with a longer time horizon, as withholding tax is levied independently of the holding period (lump sum).

Where day trading strategies mandate full closure of all positions before the close of trading, this often depends on the credit financing of the transactions.

Price fluctuations in the stock markets are small within a very short period of time. Taking transaction costs into account, it is often only possible to generate sufficient price gains with relatively high stakes.

Differences between day trading, "normal" trading, and investment

RISKS

Assuming an identical level of debt financing, day trading is not associated with a fundamentally higher risk than other investment strategies. On the contrary:

Since positions are not held overnight or over weekends, even a significant portion of the price risk is eliminated.

Irrespective of this, daytraders usually apply very narrow measures to limit losses.

EXPECTATION

Controversial are the earnings expectations in day trading. Since the 1990s, studies are published repeatedly, according to which only a small minority of the day traders generates high profits. A study by the Universities of California and Chicago, for example, concluded that of the 130,000 daytraders in Taiwan, only 500 achieved a daily return of 0.20%.

Critics of such studies contend that the existence of a sufficient number of successful daytraders as proof of the profit opportunities is sufficient - after all, the permanently successful actors in principle also used the same methods.

TIME

Day trading is not necessarily a full-time job with a permanent presence requirement on your home PC. Through the proliferation of mobile devices, access to accounts and depots is possible even on the move. In addition, a significant portion of day trading strategies is based on algorithms that can be automatically implemented as needed.

Trading Approaches

Day trading is - from its basic philosophy to its practical implementation - a fairly formal matter.

Unlike some products from Hollywood might suggest, day trading is not about insider information, "hot tips" and the "instinct" of talented actors.

Simplified, it is about the most efficient detection of meaningful patterns.

Which markets are traded?

Day trading basically affects all bond classes: equities can be traded as intraday as bonds, commodities, and foreign exchange. While there are exceptions, the majority of daytraders focus on liquid markets - blue-chip stocks, WTI crude, BUND futures, gold, FX majors, etc.

Some strategies are limited to a single underlying asset, such as e.g. the S & P 500, DAX, BUND Future or EUR / USD. Other strategies apply defined entry signals to any market that meets certain criteria in terms of liquidity, trading hours and accessibility for retail investors.

Which instruments are traded?

An important decision concerns the instruments traded. You can choose between equities, exchange-traded index funds, futures, CFDs and other derivative financial instruments such as Eg warrants and leverage certificates.

Stocks And Etfs

Securities loans are flexible and, for the most part, close to the money market with interest-bearing credit lines.

Stocks can be traded on the stock exchange and over the counter, with over-the-counter trading not recommended for day traders due to wider spreads. Shares are fundamentally not linked to a financial lever. However, this can be achieved by using a securities loan. With a securities loan, blue chips can be loaned with 50-80% of their market value.

Exchange-traded index funds are listed UCITS investment funds on an ongoing basis. For example, major indexes such as the DAX and Dow Jones. There are index funds with integrated financial leverage (eg LevDAX) and short indices, with which one can participate in falling prices. This is otherwise only possible for private investors quite cumbersome short sales.

The fees for trading in equities and index funds depend on transaction volume, broker and market.

Futures / Options

Futures contracts are in terms of liquidity, transparency. Transaction costs for day traders optimal.

Futures and options are traded on futures exchanges such as Eurex. Futures contracts are optimal in terms of liquidity, transparency and transaction costs for day traders. In addition, speculation on rising and falling prices are possible. Both futures and options are associated with leverage.

A weak point concerns the contract sizes, which are determined by the respective futures exchange for each individual underlying and despite very high margin requirements can entail very high capital requirements. Thus, Eurex lays down for DAX contracts z. For example, a value of $ 25 per index point, which at $ 10,000 points and 10% margin means $ 25,000 for a contract. Meanwhile, there is also a mini-FDax with 5 € per point, and the E-mini futures in the US are generally cheaper priced than the European futures. $

Warrants & Leverage Certificates

Warrants and leverage certificates are issued by banks in the legal form of a bearer bond and track the performance of an underlying. Leverage certificates are similar to futures. Warrants are based on options and thus much more complicated in terms of pricing. In absolute terms, the transaction costs in exchange trading are often lower than in stock trading because the integrated leverage means that the transaction volumes are lower.

Leverage certificates often have the benefit of a knock-out threshold that limits maximum loss. For this, as with the warrants, the price positions are often incomprehensible, ie the bills do not go 1: 1 with the underlying. Which makes orders very difficult based on chart technical levels.

CFDS

CFDs are traded over-the-counter, offering huge financial levers and, assuming a suitable broker, low transaction costs. In particular, equity and index CFDs with DMA brokers that settle the contracts at reasonable market prices are relevant to day traders. Since they reflect the price of the underlying 1: 1 with very low capital requirements, CFDs are ideally suited for beginners. Much more detailed information about CFDs can be found on the CFD Trading page.

Technical And Other Requirements For Day Trading

Day trading no longer requires elitist equipment, but it still requires full equipment, especially with regard to software and course supply.

Pc & Other Devices

The need for a PC with fast Internet access is self-evident. While access to the trading account with mobile devices via apps is also possible without particularly high technical standards, a stationary PC or laptop should have a certain capacity with regard to the requirements of modern trading platforms.

Special "Trader PCs" with "buy" button and multiple screens are not mandatory.

Price Data

Daytraders urgently require a complete supply of real-time push courses for all relevant markets. End-of-day data is just as inadequate as courses with a 15-minute delay. Not all brokers provide this course supply for free. The fees for course data subscriptions are sometimes reduced or refunded with sufficient trading activity.

Analysis And Order Software

Not every order mask fulfills the requirements of a daytrader. It must be possible to observe several markets in parallel and send orders in a very short time. The more order options available (trailing stop, if-done-order etc.), the better. The analysis software should also go well beyond a repertoire of drawing tools and the most common indicators.

If you have little or no programming knowledge, you have to pay attention to a large pool of functions, indicators, and strategies, which ideally can be easily combined.

Development Opportunities For Trading Systems

Sometimes it may be necessary to use third-party offerings in parallel with the software of a broker. This applies in particular with regard to development opportunities for trading systems. Here, backtesting, community, and development environment should not be enough just for beginners.

Market Scanner

Daytraders cannot investigate 24/7 all relevant markets for the possible occurrence of trading signals. One of the most important practical tools is, therefore, a market scanner (usually to be used by third-party providers). With scanners can z. For example, the German or North American stock markets are selectively searched for stocks whose indicators are close to an entry signal. These shares can then z. B. be included in a watch list.

Broker Who Allows Day Trading And Is Worth The Money

Some brokers exclude day trading or deliberately put hurdles in the way of short-term scalpers. Among all other day trading brokers, the one who has the lowest order fees for the individual transaction profile is not automatically the best.

The order fees taking into account all discounts are important for day traders, but not the only criterion. At least as much it depends on the quality of the course position and the order execution.

A price difference of z. B. 10% can certainly be justified by better performance in trading platform, order types, and automated trading.

Capital

In order to be able to live from Daytrading as an exclusive earning for a living, serious calculations require at least $500,000.

The entry barriers for day traders in terms of capital requirements have declined, not least due to the spread of CFD trading in recent years. But with a few hundred euros it is not. If a maximum of 5% of the account balance is invested per position and at the same time meaningful transaction sizes are to be achieved, $10,000 even in CFD trading, is the lower limit for day traders.

Mental And Professional Competence

Daytraders should have read more topical literature than just "Basic Information on Investing in Securities". A business degree is not necessary as well as profound programming skills. Beginners should be able to classify the daily news situation into a context that is proficient in the fundamentals of technical analysis and familiar with trading software. Trading psychology is a very complex topic, an introduction to the matter can be found here.

Trading Strategy

A trading strategy that defines entry and exit signals, as well as measures to limit losses, is mandatory for binding day trading. The second part of the series is therefore dedicated to trading strategies.

Without a trading strategy, ultimately only haphazard trading is possible "from the gut", which usually leads to higher and often irreparable losses sooner rather than later.

In the next chapter, we will talk about the basics of day trading and strategy development.

FUNDAMENTALS AND STRATEGY DEVELOPMENT OF DAY TRADING

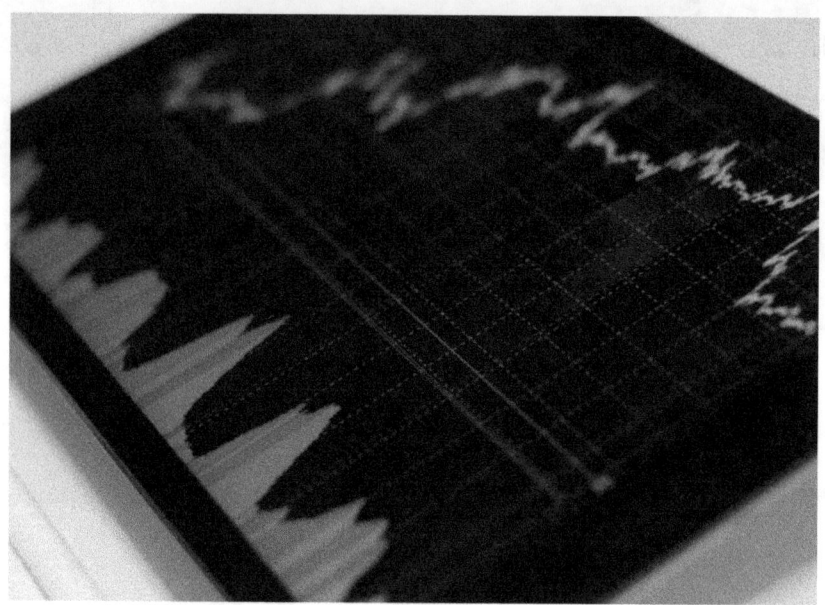

While the first chapter dealt with some basics of day trading, the second part is dedicated to the topic "day trading strategies". On the one hand, it is about the characteristics of a trading strategy in general. On the other hand, it is also about concrete examples of trading approaches.

Definition of a strategy

A trading strategy can be defined as a set of rules. The rules contain clear statements on the following questions:

- Under what circumstances are positions opened?

- Under what circumstances are positions closed?
- How much money is used and risked per trade?

A strategy determines that a position will be opened as soon as a precisely defined situation occurs in one of the considered markets.

A strategy determines that a position will be opened as soon as a precisely defined situation occurs in one of the considered markets. It may be z. B. to act a 30-day high. Very often, the entry events are additionally linked to a filter: the opening of a position occurs at a 30-day high when the trading volume is higher than on the three previous trading days.

The combination of precondition (30-day high) and filter (sales) corresponds to the definition of an entry signal.

In the context of risk and money management, it is also stipulated that 5% of the account balance will be invested if there is an initial signal (eg). "Investing" should be unequal to "risking": It must be stipulated that a stop-loss is placed in such a way that a maximum of 10% of the bet or 0.50% of the account balance in the position can be lost when opening a position , Potential risks not covered by a stop-loss should be waived here.

The stop-loss defines an exit scenario but is not an exit signal.

An exit signal defines the closure of a profitable position, as no further high profits are expected. For example, it may provide for closure of the position in the event of a significant decline in price momentum.

Features of trading strategies

There are countless trading approaches known as day trading strategies. The complexity of some of these approaches is remarkable. Beginners should, however, put to heart, what advanced have long known:

The simple strategies prove to be the best in the long run.

This has an intuitively easy to understand the reason. Day trading is about identifying markets that are in a potential phase. All entry signals are based on the recognition of some form of special activity in the market. Special activity, in turn, can be measured with relatively simple methods.

Every trading strategy has certain features. Developers can measure their strategy by these characteristics, users can search in the huge pool of circulating trading approaches specifically for desired profiles.

1. **Performance Or Profit Factor**

Performance is considered the most important feature of a strategy: the more money is earned, the better.

Performance is considered the most important feature of a strategy. In most cases, the performance in months and years is considered as well as the total return since the beginning of the application of a strategy. A high performance alone does not say anything about its composition and is therefore certainly a necessary but not sufficient condition for the existence of a good strategy.

2. **Number Of Trades**

How many trades are carried out per day, week, month and year?

A large number of trades increases transaction costs, but usually also results in a broader distribution of total profits across many individual positions. If a very large part of the overall performance is attributable to a few trades, a detailed analysis is particularly important. Chance may have played a major role in the results, which could hardly be repeated in the future. Also, the time required for the Daytrading is related to the trading activity.

3. **Payoff Ratio**

The payoff ratio is determined by dividing the average profit from profitable trades into the average loss from loss-making trades. The payoff ratio can be directly influenced by the loss limitation rules:

Ideally, the average loss does not differ significantly from the maximum risk taken on each position.

4. Trade Ratio / Hit Rate

The trade ratio indicates the ratio of profitable to loss-making trades.

The trade ratio indicates the ratio of profitable to loss-making trades and thus corresponds to the concept of "hit ratio". However, there are differences in the presentation: If 100 trades 60 are completed with a profit and 40 with a loss, this results in a trade ratio of 1.5 and a hit ratio of 60%.

The lower the hit ratio, the higher the payoff ratio must be for a strategy to be profitable.

Some strategies do not achieve many, others only a few bigger ones. It should be noted that it is only clear at the conclusion of a trade, whether this improves the hit rate or deteriorates. A very tight loss-limiting strategy can reduce the hit rate but improve outcomes.

Case Study

Case I: The trading account has a balance of $ 100,000. $ 5,000 will be invested per position. If a loss position is closed by means of a stop loss, a loss of $500 will be incurred. After 100 trades, a strategy has a hit rate of 50%. 50 trades were closed with a loss of $ 500 each and a cumulative $ 25,000. 50 trades were closed with an average profit of $ 600 and a cumulative $ 30,000. This results in a gain of 5% or 0.05% per trade.

Case II: The same strategy is trading with a narrower loss limit. Pro Trade will allow a maximum loss of $ 200 under otherwise equal conditions. This means that all positions closed by Stop Loss in Case I will continue to be closed - but additional positions not affected in Case I will be closed. The hit rate is reduced to 35%. 65 trades are closed with a loss of $200 each and a cumulative $ 13,000. 35 trades are closed with an average profit of $ 600 each and a cumulative $21,000. This results in a profit of 8% or 0.08% per trade.

1. Max. Drawdown

The maximum drawdown indicates which highest loss on a daily, weekly, monthly or yearly basis has suffered a strategy. Similarly, a maximum drawdown for the future can be defined as a "ripcord". Then the risk management can be achieved when a certain loss z. B. provide for the closure of all positions. The maximum drawdown is thus a measure of the risk that can be expected from a considered strategy.

2. Volatility

Volatility indicates the fluctuation intensity and can not only refer to markets, but also to the capital curve of a strategy.

The lower the volatility, the better.

If the capital curve runs with small fluctuations, this indicates a high hit rate, short maximum loss series, and successful risk management.

3. Sharpe Ratio

The Sharpe ratio is a measure of the excess return relative to the risk assumed. The performance of a strategy is first reduced by the safe yield of government bonds (in terms of opportunity cost) and then put into relation to volatility.

Technical Analysis for Daytrader: Where does the music play?

Fundamental data such as the economy, balance sheet profits, interest rates, etc. are not relevant for day traders - unless the events are focussed on a news trading strategy. Decisive is the technical market analysis. Daytraders require entry signals with the greatest possible precision. This can always be found where the market reveals significant changes in the relationship between supply and demand.

The basic premise of day trading is that noticeable price movements, at least for a very short period of time, result in further conspicuous market movements and that these second moves are a reaction to the initial stimuli - and thus predictable. So the key question for day traders is: Where does the music play?

New Highs And Lows As Daytrading Entry Signal

One of the classic entry signals in day trading is the appearance of new highs. For example, a new two-month high (as well as a 2-day or hour high) may be defined as the entry signal. If such strategies are used without a filter, long-term success usually lags. It is important to distinguish highs with significant significance from "noise". In practice, these filters are both the most complicated and authoritative parameter.

On the one hand, this can be achieved by looking at the trading range. The trading range of a given period (day, hour, quarter hour, etc.) should be greater than the trading margins of the three preceding periods. On the other hand, the trading volume can be considered within the period and in comparison with other periods. The volume should be greater than in the other periods and increase in the direction of the (expected) outbreak.

Trends

Trends play an important role in all temporal levels and thus also in day trading. They can be identified and measured using trendlines and indicators.

The trend is one of the most common applications.

Particularly high hit rates have trend following strategies with an additional filter, with which only stable trends are traded.

Among the best-known trend following strategies with filters is the MACD trading method. Here, a buy signal is triggered when a faster (= shorter or heavier weighted) moving average intersects a longer average from bottom to top.

Indicators

Indicators are derived in a variety of ways from price developments and play a much greater role in day trading than visual chart analysis. While the latter requires manual consideration of the market, indicators can be automatically calculated and used to generate trading signals.

The best-known indicators include moving averages with different weighting methods and interval lengths. Moving averages can also be considered as smooth trendlines and are used in numerous trading systems despite - or perhaps because of - their simple design.

Another important indicator is the Directional Movement Index (DMI), which in a smoothed variant is also called the Average Directional Movement Index (ADX). The ADX shows both the direction and the strength of a trend and is therefore often used as an upstream filter (a necessary condition) for trading strategies: One position is z. B. only opened when the ADX indicates a sufficiently strong trend.

Chart Technical Marks

Chart Marks can be used in day trading for various purposes. One way is z. For example, in opening a trend direction just above support. Likewise, positions in the direction of an outbreak via resistors are conceivable. In most day trading strategies, however, not the technical chart, but the outbreak with its concomitants (increasing volume and rising volatility) is defined as the entry signal.

Development Of An (Automated) Trading Strategy

For ambitious daytraders, the development of a trading strategy is comparable to a passion that also brings in money when it goes according to plan. Before the steps on the way to their own strategy, however, the good news for "development objectors" anticipates:

It is not absolutely necessary to learn a programming language and invest a lot of effort in a day trading strategy. There are enough ready-made strategies whose success is well documented. Easy to find z. Eg scripts for the trading platforms MT4 and MT5.

"Thoroughbred day traders" cannot be deprived of the pleasure and challenge of independent strategy development. Each strategy begins with an idea that should answer, as it were, answers to two questions:

Which recognizable events (in the chart) precede larger price movements?

How can one recognize at an early stage that it does not come to such a movement?

The answers to these two questions ultimately form the DNA of a trading strategy, because they firstly define conditions for entry and secondly make a qualitative assessment of the entry signals. The second variant decides in practice on the viability of an approach.

If these two questions are answered on the basis of own observations and considerations on markets, the essence of the strategy should fit the trader. On the other hand, if strategies are adopted without the context of personal experience, the strategy may not fit into one's own type of trading.

In the second step, the statements must be translated into objective rules that can be implemented in the form of an algorithm by a computer. This is also recommended if an automated implementation is not planned:

The more objectively and formally the criteria are defined, the more meaningful are all subsequent results, eg of backtests.

Ambitious daytraders sooner or later have to deal with programming languages. However, languages such as Equilla (similar to Visual Basic for example) or MQL5 (similarities to C ++) only have to be learned in a rudimentary form if preset indicators are mere to be combined into a trading system.

Below is an example of the code of a Moving Average Crossover system in the Equilla language used by Tradesignalonline.com, one of the largest German technical analysis and day trading communities. The code makes it easy to clarify the definition of binding rules in formal terms.

The "inputs" are two moving averages (MA) with 20 and 40 periods, respectively. An MA crossover system is based on the crossing of the slower average by the faster average. With identical weighting, the MA with a shorter number of periods (here: MA 1) is faster.

The "variables" in this case consist of the two averages with the parameters defined under "Inputs". A long signal is generated when MA1 exceeds MA2. A short signal is in the opposite case. At the same time, it is determined that the opening of a position in the form of a market order has to be made.

The trading system is incomplete in this form because it does not include exit signals. Basically, in the case of a "blind" application, an existing long position would only be neutralized if a short signal occurred and vice versa.

Following the same pattern, a trading system based on Bollinger ribbons can be constructed. In this example, the lower band serves as a trigger: If the market crosses the lower band from the bottom to the top, if there is a long-entry signal, the price falls below the lower band, a short signal is present. The parameters, in this case, are the length of the moving average and the standard deviation.

Also, this system does not provide any exit signals. It would only be possible to use only either the long or the short signals and to close the position when opposing signals occur.

Complete trading systems consist of long-entry, long-exit, short-entry and short-exit signals. This is clearly visible z. Using the MACD crossover method, whose Equilla code is shown in the screenshot below. In the default settings of most Chartig programs, the parameter settings for Daytrader are only limited. In this case, the MACD crossover system is based on 9, 12, and 26-day moving averages. However, the application is also possible with minutes or hours as period lengths.

```
MACD Crossover
 1 |Meta:
 2 |        Synopsis( "Generates trading signals when the MACD value crosses its trigger." );
 3 |
 4 |Inputs:
 5 |        Price( Close ),
 6 |        PeriodFast( 12, 1 ),
 7 |        PeriodSlow( 26, 1 ),
 8 |        Trigger( 9, 1 ),
 9 |        Bullish( LongEntry, ShortExit, NoBullishSignal ) = LongEntry,
10 |        Bearish( LongExit, ShortEntry, NoBearishSignal ) = LongExit;
11 |
12 |Variables:
13 |        macdVal, triggerVal;
14 |
15 |macdVal = MACD( Price, PeriodFast, PeriodSlow );
16 |triggerVal = XAverage( macdVal, Trigger );
17 |
18 |If Bullish <> NoBullishSignal Then
19 |        If macdVal Crosses Over triggerVal Then
20 |                If Bullish = LongEntry Then
21 |                        Buy Next Bar at Market
22 |                Else If Bullish = ShortExit Then
23 |                        Cover Next Bar at Market;
```

Backtests And Parameters In The Development Of Trading Systems

No trading system is used in practice until it has proven itself, at least on paper. With backtest programs, the rules of a trading strategy can be applied to historical prices. As a result, developers (or users, if it is a finished script) will then, at best, see what performance an algorithm has achieved in the past. The evaluation includes key figures such as performance, drawdown, etc.

Backtesting lurks a lot of pitfalls. An urgent reference to all impatient newcomers:

Backtesting does not serve as "proof" for the functioning of a strategy but as an indication of possible weaknesses. A good result in the backtest must first be validated before it can be considered valid.

This should be noted in the backtest:

The results should not change significantly with minor shifts in the parameters

If the results change with changes in the time of observation or the market considered, plausible reasons must be found

Basically, backtesting of (day trading) strategies should be carried out with a whole range of parameters and in many different markets and periods of observation. If a test with these prerequisites cannot be proved for a particular script, the developer may make a decisive mistake and lose himself in overoptimization.

As part of the backtests, a script will be adapted to a specific market and period until the paper has excellent results. In truth, however, the system has been optimized only for historical market evolution, which does not repeat itself. The informative value for the future is therefore zero.

By contrast, good trading strategies are characterized by a clear basic philosophy and simple rules that, at least in principle, work in all markets.

However, if a backtest shows that the results of the strategy largely depend on the market under consideration and/or the time period under consideration, this alone does not prove the unsuitability of the approach. Instead, root cause research is the order of the day: is there a causal relationship between the prevailing trend and the performance? If so, how does the system react to the "wrong" trend: are they not generating any trading signals or are there long losing series?

These and other questions, and above all the answers, provide the basis for further development of the strategy. In the course of development work can z. For example, point out that an initially prioritized system can be used much more effectively as a filter for another system.

Definition of exit signals and loss limitation

In practice, the formulation of a trading strategy requires further input than shown in the previous examples. In particular, it is necessary to determine how to deal with unrealized profits and losses.

How to handle book profits depends on personal preferences as well as the nature of the long exit or short exit signal. If this leaves the market after the entry "on the long line" and is generated only after relatively large price movements against the position direction, a signal for a closing position, the integration of a trailing-stop rule in the system may be useful. Then the stop-loss initially placed just below the entry price will be adjusted to rising prices at fixed intervals.

There are situations in which a position is closed, although the entry signal was not revoked by the trading strategy and the position was not closed by a stop loss. This applies to profitable positions, which are believed to have further potential.

Note: There are situations in which a position is closed, although the entry signal was not revoked by the trading strategy and the position was not closed by a stop loss. This applies to profitable positions, which are generally credited with further potential. A sudden reset is then used for profit-taking before the system generates an exit signal.

Day trading is not feasible without a loss limitation strategy. Each position must be equipped with a stop-loss, which limits the loss to a necessary minimum in case of an unfavorable course. The tolerance for losses and thus the margin between the entry price and the initial stop loss is decisive for the choice of the day trading strategy. Not every strategy can be dealt with a loss tolerance limited to 1.0 index points.

ONLINE TRADING - FAST MONEY OR HARD WORK?

Acting on the international financial markets from the couch and earning a lot of money with little effort: The expectations of the "dream job trader" could not be higher. In fact, you can make money with online trading - but only if you follow some basic rules and adjust your expectations to reality.

What is meant by "Online Trading", which processes take place in the background and which yields are realistic? What makes investors successful traders, which tools promise success and which new developments are there? These and other questions should be answered at this point.

What is online trading?

In English, "trading" stands for "trade" and does not differentiate between transactions in a market for local rarities, any hypermarket, and a fully electronic stock exchange.

In German-speaking countries, trading is also used as a generic term for active trading on the financial markets with equities, foreign exchange, futures, derivatives, ETFs or bonds. This refers to trading approaches with a short time horizon of a few months at the most and quite a few transactions.

Long-term strategies such as B. Dividend strategies, on the other hand, are more likely to fall into the category of capital investment. Accordingly, trading is primarily aimed at generating price gains by exploiting short- and medium-term market fluctuations. The long-term development of the real economy is less important than market psychology and technology.

For example, if you want to trade stocks, use the money to buy shares in a company. If the value of these shares subsequently increases, you can resell them and thus make a profit. That's the definition of trading: you buy one instrument at a certain price (or price) and sell it to another. In the optimal case, the selling price is higher and the trader makes his return from the difference between the two prices.

"Online Trading" aims to process transactions over the Internet. Private investors can place orders via the Internet via suitable brokerage. This is possible from any computer in the world with little time and at low transaction costs. But not only the transactions but also the procurement and evaluation of market-relevant information is possible via the Internet.

"Online Trading" is now a synonym for "Trading", since order placement and information gathering are largely done via the Internet anyway.

How does a stock exchange work and how are traders connected to it?

But how can profits be made with short-term price fluctuations? To understand this, it is first necessary to look at how a stock exchange works. Stock exchanges are central trading venues on which supply and demand for securities converge.

Stock Exchange Participants As Intermediaries

As a private investor, you yourself can not place any orders directly in the trading system of a stock exchange. This is only possible through exchange participants - ie banks and brokers. They provide their customers (which not only include private investors but also investment companies and other institutional investors) with order masks and accept orders via the Internet. In the case of buy orders, the trading participants also check whether the liquidity on your custody account/clearing account is sufficient.

Transaction Costs Are Retained By The Broker

The broker will be informed about the execution of the order and will then credit your clearing account with the sales proceeds minus transaction costs (sales order) or charge the purchase price plus order fees and post the acquired securities into your securities account.

Low Hurdles For Getting Started With Online Trading

Private investors can submit a large number of orders per day via the Internet. Even the purchase and sale of a security within a trading day (intraday trading or day trading) is - if the broker does not rule this out in its provisions - easily possible. In addition to some money, online trading, therefore, requires no more than a service contract with a broker, which is concluded with the opening of a securities account.

When will online trading become profitable?

Making money can be achieved through active exchange trading when a sufficiently large proportion of the transactions ends in a profit. These profits must first cover the "operating costs" of online trading: the inevitable losses and the transaction costs. Only when the profits go well beyond, online trading becomes a profitable venture.

Trading - art, craft or illusion?

Critics of active trading often argue that financial market performance is either accidental or based on extremely complex and unpredictable mechanisms, so any attempt to gain in value with fluctuations will be doomed to failure.

If that were true, online trading would be nothing but a business model of brokers for clients who might as well try gambling. However, the opposite has been proven for decades: It is possible to make lasting and systematic profits by deliberately speculating on price changes. This possibility exists because courses are not random, but move within recognizable laws of the market.

These patterned market movements occur along with sudden and nonspecific movements. Online trading is about identifying meaningful constellations and exploiting them for profitable trades. This requires less an artistic talent than analytical thinking. But you do not have to reinvent the wheel for the second time: In order to be able to anticipate and anticipate price movements, knowledge in the area of technical market analysis is helpful. Most short- and medium-term strategic approaches are based on this discipline.

The Technical Analysis And Its Importance For Private Investors

For Technical Analysis (TA) who still considers neither corporate earnings growth, but only the price development of security. The TA has been used since the end of the 19th century and assumes that all relevant information is already included in the course. It also assumes that prices are moving in trends and patterns and that trends are consistent, ie not subject to mere coincidence.

The Three Biggest Advantages Of Technical Analysis:

- It is easy to learn.
- The technical analysis works the same for every market.

- It requires very little resources, most of which are freely accessible.

The Technical Analysis makes it relatively easy to determine the state of a market and its likely direction of movement.

A simple example:

If the market is at the bottom of an intact uptrend channel, it is likely that the price will rise. Just looking at trends, resistance, and support, as well as simple price information, often enough allows an assessment of the market. Many brokers provide charting software to private investors, which allows most TA tools to be used.

Basic knowledge is often provided in the context of free or low-priced webinars, in which at best with close practical relevance to the current technical condition of important markets is analyzed. Beginners, assuming they have a personal assignment, should be able to learn the basic skills of the TA within a few months.

What is required in online trading?

A PC with an Internet connection or a corresponding mobile device are therefore sufficient for both the transmission of orders and the analysis of the market. Online trading requires neither a degree in business administration nor a bank education. Also extensive equipment such. B. PCs with multiple screens is not required for beginners and advanced users.

How to earn money with Online Trading?

A trading strategy is a well-defined set of rules that produces entry and exit signals.

Money is generated in online trading through the consistent implementation of trading strategies. Such strategies can be developed on their own or adopted from a large pool of freely available approaches. Beginners and advanced learners with no experience in developing and validating strategies are generally better served with ready-made approaches; Over time, successful traders usually develop the ambition to develop their own strategies.

A trading strategy is nothing more than a clearly defined set of rules that produces entry and exit signals. The regulations are based on observations of market situations, which are considered to have a sufficiently high forecasting power with regard to further market development. A very simple example to implement is breakout strategies. If a market breaks resistance or support or breaks out of a chart formation (eg head-and-shoulders formation), a position is opened in the direction of expected market development.

Proven trading strategies are not complicated

For the implementation of outbreak strategies, a screening is first required that can relate to one market or a number of different markets. At the same time, markets are already relevant if the indications of an imminent outbreak are condensed. This is z. For example, when a market is moving in the direction of significant resistance.

In the second step, the strategy takes effect: it determines the circumstances under which a position is opened. This may be the case, for example, if the market close of a market is at least 1.0% above significant resistance. This definition is more than just a detail: the exact definition decisively determines the "hit rate".

If a position is opened too soon after the alleged breakthrough by technical resistance, the risk of a "false alarm" and an ultimately unsustainable outbreak is great. On the other hand, if you start too late, it will diminish the potential of each individual position.

Trading strategy defines entry and exit in online trading

The optimization of these parameters is based on empirical evidence, not only in terms of outbreak strategies. These can be applied in the context of backtesting with suitable software (which, for example, can be free in the case of MetaTrader).

The detailed implementation of a strategy is simulated on the basis of historical price progressions and the hypothetical performance is measured. Based on marginal changes to the parameters, this procedure can be used to determine which settings would have achieved the highest yield in the past. From this, concrete conclusions can be drawn for future applications.

Trading strategies not only define the right time to enter the market but also determine the exit.

When opening a position, the initial exit price initially results from the definition of loss limitation: Usually, the maximum loss per position is limited by a stop loss, which is triggered automatically when a set price level is reached.

For example, you buy one share at the asking price of $ 103.50 and place a stop loss at $ 98.00 at the same time. As soon as the bid price, reaches a level, a sell order is automatically triggered.

Set on rising and falling courses - without a constant presence on the screen

If the price rises after the share purchase, the stop-loss level can be gradually raised. As a result, already started, but not yet realized profits are protected against price reset.

As an alternative to manual adjustment, a trailing stop loss can be installed. This is a stop-loss order whose triggering price is adjusted to rising market rates at fixed intervals. It is also possible to enter a market automatically without constant observation by issuing a stop-buy order: this triggers a buy order when a specified price level is reached.

A major difference between investment and active trading is the ability to bet on falling prices. Private investors have at their disposal various instruments and securities such as short sales, short certificates, put warrants and CFDs.

Analysis, costs, course supply: The Internet has reduced the barriers to entry

Successful traders do not need insider knowledge (which is already prohibited in the application anyway) and can observe, analyze and trade relevant markets without high costs and time.

The combination of charting software, intelligent order types and mobile access to securities accounts has reduced the barriers to active trading. Online trading is possible for just about anyone who can invest a few hours a week - depending on the strategy chosen, even less is needed.

A significant number of brokers provide their clients with a complete solution for online trading: In addition to their own trading and administrative functions (order placement, performance statistics, etc.), the trading platforms also include applications in the field of charting and analysis, including price data supply and, in many cases, development opportunities and the use of automated trading systems.

The Internet has also paved the way for low-cost brokers so that the transaction costs in exchange and OTC trading have declined significantly since the turn of the millennium. This also applies to trade on foreign stock exchanges. CFD and FX brokers have also helped to reduce the barriers to online trading.

Private investors can use these brokers to trade many previously hard-to-reach markets (commodities, precious metals, etc.) - four-digit deposits are enough to leverage. The strong growth in the supply of ETPs (exchange-traded products, such as exchange-traded index funds and hedged commodity certificates) has also broadened the scope of private investors for short-term exposures.

THE SUCCESSFUL TRADERS

What skills characterize successful traders?

The entry barriers to online trading are lower than ever since there are financial markets. Nevertheless, a PC with an Internet connection and the latest analysis software alone will not make you a successful trader.

As such, you are essentially pursuing one goal: you are trying to generate a significantly higher return than you would expect with a simple buy and hold equity strategy. If you succeed permanently, you are already a successful trader. But what qualities and skills do you need to become a successful trader?

> **Learning And Experience**

Online trading does not require a science degree. Nevertheless, profound basic knowledge is helpful. In particular, in-depth knowledge of equities and derivatives and sufficient knowledge and practical skills in the field of technical analysis are required. They should also understand why a warrant can sometimes be "strange" and able to identify the prevailing market trend, significant resistance and support zones, and price formation.

The latter is demonstrated in the visually often much less clear practice and not in the textbook theory. You should also know all the tactical order types and their uses. At least as important as the willingness to learn is your willingness to take on a new role. As a trader, you are no longer just a consumer of financial news in TV, magazines and the Internet, commenting on what's happening in the personal comfort zone, essentially against yourself. As a trader, you are right in the middle of it and directly affected by many events.

> **Mental Strength And Stamina**

Not a few newcomers are confronted for the first time in their lives with autonomous decisions with regard to financial investments - apart from the decision between passbook and fixed deposit.

If a substantial portion of private wealth is used, mental pressure inevitably builds up and you will sooner or later have to cope with it. Try to answer the following questions as honestly as possible.

How do you react if your trading strategy produces a longer losing series?

Do you have any beliefs about trading strategies and long-term success when a colleague with a "secret tip" "earns" 70% in a week?

Could you develop an avoidance behavior towards your computer because you want to instinctively hide the reality of lost or lost profits?

Are ranked lists of friends and colleagues more important to you than your personal goals?

Do you continue your efforts in terms of expertise and development if the first year of online trading produced only mediocre results?

And last but not least: do you hope for the online trading thrill, as in Hollywood films on "Wall Street"?

Whether you have what it takes to become a successful trader depends on your answers to these questions. Successful traders can make significant profits in virtually any market situation, leaving conventional equity investments, etc., far behind.

The basis of this success, however, is neither innate talent nor outstanding cognitive abilities, but rather the ability to suffer (apprenticeship!) And perseverance. Online trading in practice is a pretty sober affair that has much to do with discipline and cool analysis/evaluation and little with drama.

Success In Trading: The Four "Secrets" Of Successful Traders

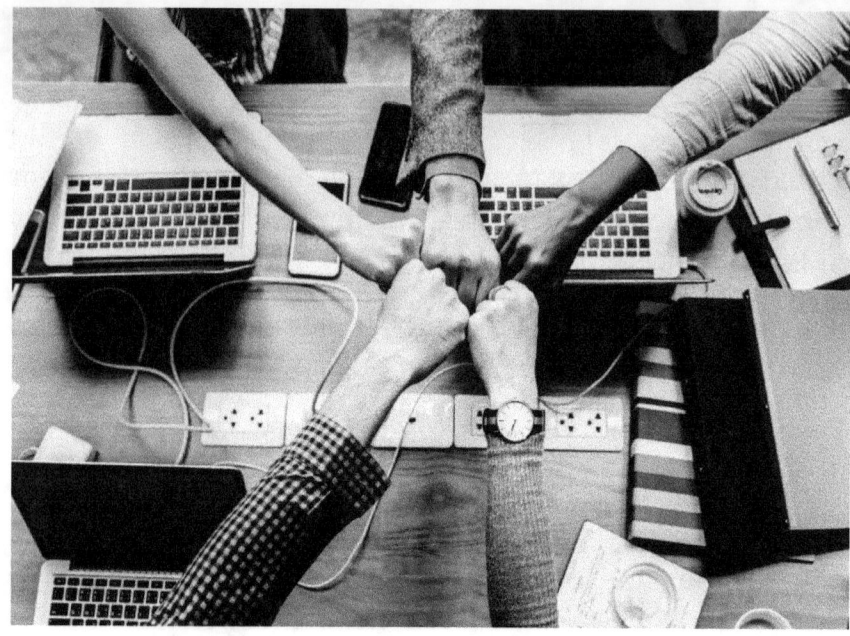

In the following, the properties mentioned in the previous section will be translated into concrete success factors and instructions for action. If successful traders are asked about their "secrets", disillusionment quickly ensues among the questioners: everyone could have come up with the supposedly super strategies themselves.

> ➢ **Stick To Your Strategy**

There is no substitute for a conceptually meaningful trading strategy with concrete measures for limiting losses - if necessary through a portfolio with more than one such strategy. Keep in mind that no occasion can be worth deviating from the cool-headed strategy.

Promising market constellations are recognized early enough by a good strategy, leaving dangerous situations early enough due to exit. Online trading is based on analytical considerations that are never bettered in the heat of the moment than after the close.

Those who act without a strategy, go into the hands of chance.

> ➢ **Capital Preservation Is The Top Priority**

Especially beginners often believe that the most successful traders are characterized by the highest possible return.

That's only half the story: the best traders in terms of professionalism achieve high, but consistently realistic returns, limiting the risk they take.

Learn to think like the "strong hands": The top priority is capital preservation. For average private wealth, this bid is visible in the very pictorial recovery effect: If 10% of the stake is lost, a loss of just over 11% is required to neutralize the loss.

At 20% loss it is already 25% profit, at 50% loss 100% and at 90% 1,000%. In other words, if you want to be successful in the long term, you have to be (long) in the long run!

> ➢ **Use only the best instruments tools - and as many as possible**

It is amazing how much performance is dispensed with by choosing an inappropriate broker. If the average cost per trade is only $ 5.00 higher than necessary due to order fees, spreads and financing costs, this will neutralize an annual return of 6% for 100 trades per month and $ 100,000 in account volume.

Therefore, look for the cheapest possible broker and take into account the foreseeable trading activity of your individual strategy. You should also use all the tools that are available and could be useful.

This applies to supposedly exotic and dispensable order types such as stop-buy-limit as well as guaranteed stop-loss orders, mobile access, etc.

> **Practice Patience - And Awe**

Do not weaken your chances of success by overly high expectations. If you can survive the first year of online trading without major losses, the foundation for a successful future is probably already laid - just by avoiding any beginner mistakes, better analytical skills, and carefully sorted information sources, chances are you'll see a significant second-year performance gain Well.

The first (very) big profits are a test. Do not lift off now and be aware that the profit is not yours but your strategy and that it will continue to be the foundation of your success.

THE 10 GOLDEN TIPS THAT EVERY TRADER SHOULD KNOW

The following rules should not be taken as a guarantee of success on the stock exchanges, because they do not exist. When trading often decide their own talent and the right sense of the success of trading decisions and there can be no guidance. Rather, these tips are designed to provide you with the optimal framework for successful trading that will help you focus on your talent.

> ➤ **It can not be done without discipline**

Do not let failures and streaks of profit influence you and act according to purely objective criteria. It's best to make a trading plan in advance and stick to it in any case. Without discipline, you will quickly lose your capital and only the broker will benefit from your wrong decisions.

> ➢ **Lose wants to be learned**

Even the best traders lose again and again, and that's why it's important to learn how to lose. A high loss must not affect subsequent trade decisions, because who acts emotionally will in most cases lose more in the long run than win.

> ➢ **Money management is essential**

As mentioned in point 1, you should set certain parameters before you start trading. Consider the amount of capital invested, how you allocate the total capital, and carefully consider the risk parameters. Here comes the discipline again, because for long-term success, it is imperative not to deviate from the set rules.

> ➢ **Never underestimate the risk**

Especially if you trade in particularly volatile markets, stops can be the life insurance for your capital. With order additions, you can partially automate your trading and are always protected against unpleasant surprises. As part of risk management, you should also ask yourself other questions, such as the opportunity-to-risk ratio (CRV) or how high the risk you are willing to bear.

> ➢ **Define your trading goals**

You should realize what goals you want to set when trading. It is important to have no exaggerated expectations of the possible profits but to plan quite realistically. Define clear entry and exit points and thus avoid hectic action during actual trading.

> **Try not only to see the hit rate**

It is not crucial that you close every trade with profit, it is much more crucial to find a suitable CRV. There are, for example, the 3: 1 rule. It is important to enter only trades that have a risk/reward ratio of 3: 1. For example, if your goal is a 15 percent return opportunity and the risk is 5 percent, you'll still see consistent capital growth with the 3: 1 rule, even if the hit rate is only 50 percent.

> **Pay attention to duplicability**

Every successful trader needs tactics, patterns, and setups that can be duplicated and thus widely used in practice. The right market technology decides to a large extent on the success of your strategies and so the duplicability should never be underestimated.

> **Be patient**

It can sometimes take a long time for a market opportunity to emerge, and especially beginners tend to become impatient and randomly place trades in order to participate in the marketplace. However, those who learn to wait for the right set-up will be more successful in the long term than someone who acts impatiently.

> **Act on your own plan**

If trading is more than a hobby for you and you are looking for a professional career, then you should see the wider path as one big whole, as a business that you want to plan carefully and consistently pursue. The daily battle for profit requires all the stops that exist and your middlemen will not let you have their capital without a fight. However, if you follow a very personal strategy and develop your own way of trading, you will not go down in the shark tank of global trading.

> **Have emotions under control**

If you follow all the above tips, you will not face any problems in daily trading. However, one of the most important points to keep in mind here should be mentioned. Always leave out all your emotions. Frustration or greed are factors that should not play a role in your decisions. Do not place trades on your stomach, because such an approach would only have one consequence - the loss of your capital.

STOCK MARKET: DEFINITION, CHARACTERISTICS, AND IMPORTANCE

To understand what the stock market is, it is necessary to go much further than the definition itself. Therefore, in this book, we will touch on various aspects and components that actively participate in it.

Then you will know more about all these aspects, but let's start at the beginning:

What are the stock markets?

The definition of the stock market corresponds to that of a type of capital market where equity and fixed income are traded, through the sale of negotiable securities. Something that allows channeling the capital of investors and users in the medium and long term.

The issuance, placement and distribution process depends on the participants that are the issuers, investors, intermediaries and other economic agents.

Negotiable securities issued by individuals or entities, whether public or private, are also affected in the process. They are for example negotiable securities: shares of companies and negotiable securities equivalent to shares, participative shares of savings banks, securitization bonds, mortgage participations, monetary marketing instruments, preferred shares, warrants, among others.

Likewise, options contracts, term interest rate agreements and other financial instrument contracts related to securities, financial instruments, raw materials, etc. are considered negotiable securities.

Characteristics of the stock market

Among the most important characteristics of the stock market can be found the following:

1. **Profitability:** By investing in the stock market you expect to obtain a return for this.

2. **Security:** We are talking about an equity market. This means that the values can change up or down, as the market oscillates. As is evident, this represents a risk, since it is not known with certainty whether the investment will result in a profit. Investments in long-term securities are more likely to be a profitable and

secure investment. Another way to reduce risk when investing is diversification. In this way the probability of having losses decreases.

3. **Liquidity:** There is great ease in investing in securities, so buying and selling occur quickly.

Importance of the stock market

The main objective of the stock market is to help the movement of capital, thus contributing to monetary and financial stability. This is how the democratic use of securities markets promotes the development of more active and safer monetary policies.

In this way, securities markets become places where intermediary agents and developed instruments exchange assets with each other. What facilitates transparency and freedom of the process of purchases and sales of securities.

In them, it is also possible to set the prices of the securities according to the order of the corresponding law of supply and demand. This can also be a very liquid investment for many investors because regardless of the time, they can sell their shares.

Role of securities markets

In summary, the stock market is of great importance in the national and international economic because it has the following functions:

– Contributes to economic development by channeling savings into investment.

- It provides liquidity to the investment, allowing the holders of securities to convert their shares into money.

- It puts in contact with the companies and the entities of the State that need resources of investment of savers.

- They favor the valuation of financial assets and the efficient allocation of resources.

How the stock market works

The stock market is a set of financial institutions and agents that negotiate on the different types of assets, such as stocks, bonds, funds, etc. All this using as means the instruments created specifically for this purpose.

It works by capturing in part the personal and business savings, an extra point of financing for those companies that are in processes such as the issuance of new shares.

Unfortunately, the stock market is also subject to speculation. They move a lot of actions every day, around the world, in order to achieve a surplus value for the sale of securities.

But trading on the stock market is subject to the risks of economic cycles, in addition to suffering the effects of psychological phenomena that are capable of raising or reducing the prices of securities and stocks. For what is considered an instrument to measure the impact of all those political, economic and social events that society can go through.

This is how it becomes a barometer of the behavior of economies in countries around the world. There is its most representative importance.

What are the primary and secondary markets?

The primary market and the secondary market are two types of contracting and trading that differ from each other to a large extent. Taking into account this, we have the following definitions and differences:

Primary market

The primary market is the placement or exit to the market of new shares. This means that the shares are coming directly from the company and that normally they are sold through an auction.

The sale is given either in a public bidding or direct negotiation. And in case it happens indirectly, when financial intermediaries interfere, it can be done in three ways, which are:

- **Firm sale:** Regardless of whether all the shares are sold or not is a closed deal, with a firm sale closes a number of shares for a certain amount.

- **Stand-by agreement:** This is the most common form among several financial intermediaries that manage securities simultaneously. A pre-agreement between the issuing company and the intermediary is closed. The intermediary makes sales in multiple batches and closes more share packages as needed to expand the number of the company.

- **Best Effort:** It is a direct commission sale between intermediaries. The commission earned by the companies issuing these shares is based on the sale price.

- **Gray Market:** Its name is due to the fact that it is about the employment of certain parts of the market that companies do not use as usual. Although they are not illegal, it is an unexplored market, so the knowledge of their actual result is uncertain.

- **Private Placement:** They are issued shares that are located in the private market to one or several persons in a private but direct way.

Secondary market

The secondary market is the market where the securities that have already been issued and sold in the primary market are handled in real time by sellers and buyers. Something that happens simultaneously and is executed by direct operations or corresponding financial intermediaries.

Therefore, the secondary market is the place where purchase and sale operations are carried out. These are the ones that transform the economic fabric and financial productivity from a perspective of investment and trust.

What is traded in the stock market?

In the stock market not only proceed to hire shares but also to negotiate other financial assets such as bonds, bonds, and subscription rights. That is all these financial assets that companies have decided to sell or negotiate for financing needs they have.

Differences between fixed income and variable income

These negotiated products are divided into two large groups, which are those denominated as fixed income or variable income. The type of income will depend on whether the return received by the investor is predetermined or not, respectively.

In the fixed income, you can find the debt, and the shares corresponding to the second group, to the variable income.

This last modality is preferred by companies when it is necessary to obtain financing through the stock exchange.

There are also hybrid products that are a mixture of the above, as is the case of bonds convertible into shares. They first generate a fixed interest and then transform into equity securities. Another type is obligations with warrants, with which the investor obtains the right to a premium or the conversion into another financial asset as well.

Therefore, when a person buys a variable income security, an action in a certain company, for example, does not have specific knowledge of the benefits that it will obtain. This situation occurs because he is not lending money to be returned, but with the purchase, he becomes the owner of a part of said company. It happens to be, therefore, a risky investment.

A situation opposite to that which occurs when an investor buys fixed-income security with a fixed interest rate. Doing so knows the kind of performance you will get with a predetermined time period.

It is important to highlight that in the financial market not all the equity securities listed have the same prestige. This is because they do not share the same results accounts and the same expectations. This is how some values will have more prestige than others if they are compared.

And it should also be noted that there are

Ordinary shares and preferred shares

Ordinary shares are securities that do not possess any type of special right that is further from those provided for in the law and equal in the company's bylaws. It is the ordinary shares that are in the capacity to confer the same rights to all their owners without there being any kind of distinction.

On the other hand, **preferred shares** are those that grant their holders or owners some kind of special right. As an example, it can be cited that if a corporation goes bankrupt it will be the shareholders and owners who will charge last. This is because in front of them are the creditors and within the shareholders, the preferred securities are free to collect before the rest.

Participants of the stock market

In the stock markets, a quite extensive participatory system is developed that includes multiple factors. This is how the main participants in this market are:

The issuers of securities

The issuers of securities represent those companies or trusts that offer securities issues for sale with the purpose of attracting savings from the investing public. This to finance your investments or also to obtain working capital.

The issuers can be fixed income or variable income. Fixed income issuers are securities issued by public companies or public institutions and represent loans that they receive through investors. They confer nothing more than economic rights.

This type of values determines their interests based on various indicators; other interest rates such as TBP, Prime, etc.; stock indexes such as S & P, DOW, IBEX, CAC, etc.; coupons; zero-coupon; among others.

The issuers of variable income are those that are identified as being assets of the aliquot part of the capital. Your performance is determined according to the benefits that you obtain from the fund or the company. Examples of this are the holdings and shares of investment funds.

Investment fund management companies

These are the companies that serve to manage investment funds. They have specialized people in this field.

Stock Exchange

They are entities that provide means for the purchase and sale of securities, exercising positions of authorization, regulation, inspection and on the positions of the stock exchange. Among its functions are:

- establish purchase and sale procedures
- conduct remote reviews of stock market taxes
- offer the public information about the values
- ensure the transparency of price formation

Stock positions

The stock exchange positions are entities that are authorized to perform intermediation activities in the stock market. Other functions include buying and selling securities on behalf of their clients, managing individual investment portfolios and advising the investor in the purchase and sale of securities on the stock market.

Investors

Investors or investors are the people who have resources for the acquisition of shares, bonds or other securities, and who are in the search to obtain profits from their investments.

Custody entities

Custody entities are responsible for providing services for the conservation of securities and cash in relation to them. It is also your mission to register your ownership. As well as the return to the owner, securities of the same issuer and the same characteristics that have been delivered for safekeeping.

Risk rating agencies

The risk rating companies are the entities that are authorized to issue risk ratings of the securities. These ratings are merely technical and objective opinions about the payment capacity of an issuer. They are expressed through a scale of letters and numbers.

Price providers

When talking about price providers, we talk about corporations that are authorized to professionally provide calculation services, as well as provision of valuation prices for financial instruments.

Trust companies

They are entities that have been created for the administration of trusts, in turn, they are subject to the inspection of the financial superintendence.

Entitlement companies

These entities are in charge of managing special purpose vehicles such as universals, securitization funds, and trusts. By means of which the corresponding securitization processes are structured.

Examples of stock market

Clear examples of the most important securities markets are the NASDAQ and the IBEX 35, of which we will speak a bit below:

NASDAQ

The NASDAQ (National Association of Securities Dealers Automated Quotation) is the second largest automated and electronic stock exchange in the United States and is the first in New York. Its size is such that its exchange volume per hour is greater than that of any stock exchange in the world.

In NASDAQ there are more than 7000 shares that are listed. The participating companies are characterized by having a profile of high technology, information technology, and biotechnology. It has its main office in New York and its most representative indexes are the Nasdaq 100 and the Nasdaq Composite.

IBEX 35

It is made up of the 35 companies with the most liquidity in the Electronic Stock Market Interconnection System (SIBE) of four Spanish stock exchanges, which are the Madrid Stock Exchange, Barcelona Stock Exchange, Bilbao Stock Exchange, and Valencia Stock Exchange.

This index is weighted by stock market capitalization, similar to indexes such as the S & P 500 where not all companies have the same weight. For the inclusion or exit of the IBEX 35, the following is taken into account:

- the liquidity of the securities
- the value of the market capitalization
- the number of shares outstanding, among others.

These criteria are regulated by the TAC (Technical Advisory Committee) that meets every 6 months in an ordinary manner.

THE 7 BEST INVESTMENT BOOKS FOR BEGINNERS

Investing in the stock market has never been easy, but even less so in this time of crisis, in which the ups and downs of the national and global economy cause markets to scare investors every other day. Despite this, the low-interest rates offered by banks today means that many savers choose to try to increase their profits through equities and, within that, in products linked to the stock markets. These are assets that allow us to improve the profitability of our investments but, as a counterpart, they present a level of risk that is much higher than the one that can be assumed, for example, fixed income.

That is why we must be very cautious before entering the parquet. Once inside, diversify, correct the selection of values and perform active management are key to achieve profitability that in case of success can reach two digits.

Although in networks it is common to find supposed gurus who promise success, the truth is that nobody - absolutely nobody - has a magic wand that allows him to guarantee that he will make money in the Stock Exchange. Investors should keep in mind that investment in the stock market is a risky investment in which the same way that can be earned can also be lost. Therefore, before entering into the difficult world of parquet, not only is it advisable, but it is practically obligatory, to spend time reading books that allow us to better understand the functioning of the markets.

There are many recommended readings that exist, both for people who want to enter the stock market for the first time and for those who already have experience and want to expand their knowledge. We collect some of these books in these lines. Reading it will not guarantee us making money, but it will make it easier for us to better understand the markets and how it works so that we have greater possibilities of obtaining successful investments.

1. The Intelligent Investor by Ben Graham

This 1949 book focused on Graham's strategy of loss minimization over profit maximization. This is the basic foundation of a Rule #1 education and is a good investing book for beginners. Buffett wrote a preface and appendix to the 2006 edition.

This classic text is annotated to update Graham's timeless wisdom for today's market conditions.

The greatest investment advisor of the twentieth century, Benjamin Graham, taught and inspired people worldwide. Graham's philosophy of "value investing" — which shields investors from substantial error and teaches them to develop long-term strategies — has made The Intelligent Investor the stock market bible ever since its original publication in 1949.

2. One Up On Wall Street: How To Use What You Already Know To Make Money In The Market

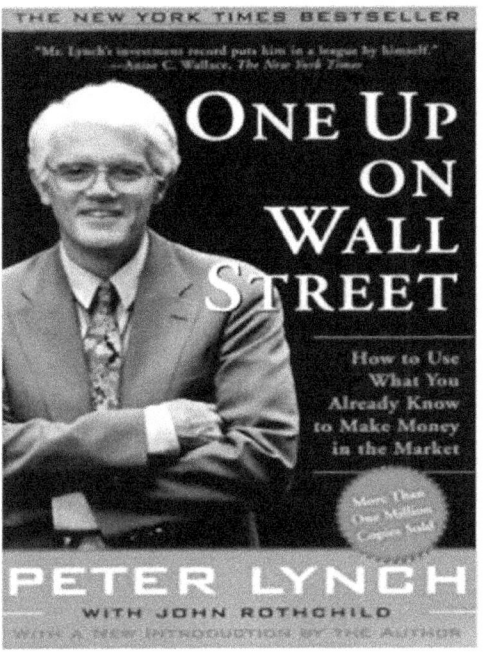

The bestseller One Up On Wall Street was written by Peter Lynch. Peter Lynch is the famed Fidelity mutual fund manager and noted philanthropist that made a fortune for his clients with the Fidelity Magellan Fund. Lynch advises investors to use their knowledge and personal experiences to find investment opportunities. Lynch's theory is "invest in what you know." One Up On Wall Street is built on the concept that the average investor can outperform the market. The average investor has an advantage over the market because they can spot undervalued opportunities in their daily life. Many of Lynch's best investment ideas were found outside of Wall Street. It is an excellent book and is a very easy read.

3. The Little Book of Common Sense Investing: The Only Way to Guarantee Your Fair Share of Stock Market Returns

Investing is all about common sense. Owning a diversified portfolio of stocks and holding it for the long term is a winner's game. Trying to beat the stock market is theoretically a zero-sum game (for every winner, there must be a loser), but after the substantial costs of investing are deducted, it becomes a loser's game. John C. ("Jack") Bogle is the founder of the Vanguard Group and creator of the world's first index fund, and The Little Book of Common Sense Investing is a top recommendation of Warren Buffett's. There's actually a funny story that when Jack Bogle first met Warren Buffett, Jack recognized Warren, went up and introduced himself, and he said to Warren, "you know the thing I really like about you is you have rumpled suits just the same as I do" - and Jack and Warren have been good friends ever since.

4. The Essays of Warren Buffet by Lawrence Cunningham

If The Intelligent Investor is the value investor's bible, then The Essays of Warren Buffett are the value investor's New Testament. Warren Buffett has been writing essays on investing and business for 50 years, and his genius - combined with his down-to-earth charm and clear prose - makes him perhaps one of the greatest educators as well as one of the greatest investors to have ever lived. Many of these essays can be found for free online, but The Essays of Warren Buffett by Lawrence Cunningham brings them all together under one roof.

5. Simple But Not Easy: An Autobiographical Book about Investing by Richard Oldfield

Simple But Not Easy has plenty of interest to the experienced professional and is aimed also at the interested amateur investor. The theme of the book is that investment is simpler than non-professionals think it is in that the rudiments can be expressed in ordinary English, and picked up by anybody.

6. Irrational Exuberance by Robert Shiller

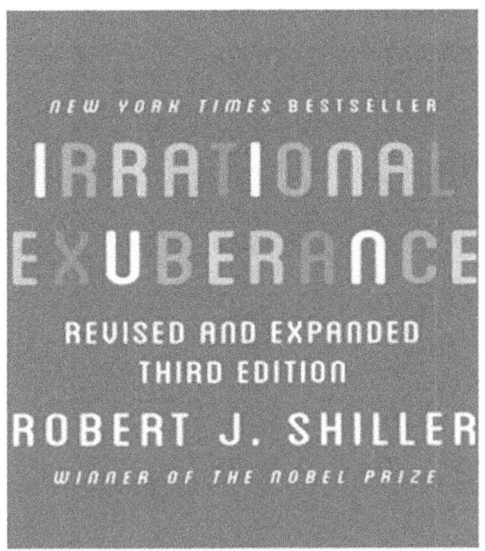

Nobel Prize-winning economist Robert Shiller, who warned of both the tech and housing bubbles, cautions that signs of irrational exuberance among investors have only increased since the 2008–9 financial crisis. With high stock and bond prices and the rising cost of housing, the post-subprime boom may well turn out to be another illustration of Shiller's influential argument that psychologically driven volatility is an inherent characteristic of all asset markets. In other words, Irrational Exuberance is as relevant as ever.

7. The Education of a Value Investor: My Transformative Quest for Wealth, Wisdom, Enlightenment by Guy Spier

This book traces the arc of a transformation. Author Guy Spier started his career as a Gordon Gekko wannabe — brash, short-sighted and entirely out for himself. Then, a series of transformations and self-realization led him from an investment banking job with a third-rate firm to managing his own fund, which has generated tremendous returns for his investors.

6 MYTHS ABOUT THE STOCK MARKET THAT CAN RUIN YOU

Do you want to start without falling into the trap? to progress quickly? Are you tired of losing all your hard earned winnings in an instant? Do you want to win regularly and without stress? So let me teach you all you need to know to finally cross a course in your trading and never be the same investor again.

When the stock market goes up we see that it is attracting more and more new investors. Unfortunately, most of these budding investors come up with a lot of stereotypes and dreams of fortune. There are many ways in which newcomers fall, and some experienced investors sometimes fall back into it as well. The stock market is a complicated world with a changing environment. It is necessary to constantly question oneself. Unfortunately, most stock market investors have a judgment that is often biased by myths. Myths that make the wealth of those who play on it for you to buy such service or training.

1. **The first myth to denounce is that you too can be Warren Buffet!**

The answer is no. You can try to invest like him, buy and hold, but the reality is that the environment today is different, you do not have the same starting capital and that Warren Buffet is a genius, certainly, but a genius who knew how to invest in the market at the right time. I no longer believe in buy and hold, I believe in buying and selling trends over periods of a few weeks to 8 months. The passive buy-and-hold investment can only operate with large capital and a large share of liquidity that allows the positions to be pyramidized. Unfortunately, 99.99999% of investors will never invest like Warren Buffet. Tell you that companies that quote below their own bottom, there are many, and many also continued to list lower and lower despite this. Warren Buffet is a genius, he must be respected but not idolized.

2. **An investment fund with high fees earns more**

It is a myth to think that a management or investment fund that levies high fees, is necessarily more efficient than the low cost. Many funds cannot beat the market or a simple index tracker. High fees do not presage quality.

3. **To win the stock market only fundamental analysis counts**

To win in dump most investors think that it is easy and that it is enough to buy companies which have good results. this is called fundamental analysis. But the stock market is not that simple, otherwise, prices would only move when the results are released. So some will tell you that only the technical analysis counts in you out a battery of technical indicators. All that is complicated is to banish. the reality is that to win the stock market you have to know how to handle graphical analysis and understand the psychology of crowds. The psychology of the crowds is inscribed in the prices of a stock and its movements. The graphical analysis coupled with the fundamental of the box will allow you to know whether to buy or sell but especially when. It is a myth to think that there is a technique based on fundamental or technical analysis that is better than the other. The truth is that we must privilege the price, just the price. There is no standard Holy Grail method.

4. **Having more than 15 positions in the portfolio helps smooth the risk**

This will especially smooth the performance and enrich your broker or banker with fees and commissions. It is important not to have all your eggs in one basket, but to disperse and worse, because you will lose performance, costs, speed, and decision-making flexibility. It is important not to have more than 8 stocks in the portfolio to be active and reduce the share of costs.

5. The stock market will make me rich easily

I know a few people who have become rich in the stock market. This can certainly improve daily life. But unless you spend some time there and treat it as a full-time job, do not expect to get rich fast. It is an everyday job and effort to not lose money.

6. You have to be better than others and beat the market

Many investors think that what is important is to measure their performance to others in order to become the best investor. It is putting huge pressure on you and so, in the end, it is counterproductive. The goal in the stock market must be to earn more money than to lose. After each year, you will find investors who have been better able to negotiate the year than you or investors who have beaten the market while you do not. The important thing is the long term and year after year, your account grows. The stock market is a marathon, not a hundred meters. You are more interested in investors whom year after year make results than shooting stars who make a sudden and then nothing.

THE STOCK TRADING SOFTWARE 2019 - THE BEST PROVIDERS AND THEIR SOFTWARE IN COMPARISON

The stock trading software facilitates all activities related to stock trading. There is a variety of stock trading software that is able to track all eligible stocks and recognize price changes in a timely manner. Suppliers such as online platforms and brokers provide their services and corresponding software. The software ensures the transparency of the price development, the trading volume and also provides information on the price-earnings ratio of certain stocks. The trader is well informed in every area.

Some well-known stock trading software

- JStock,
- Shareholder standard.

The JStock software provides an overview of the current interesting shares, in addition, the available shares can be clearly arranged. Stock prices in approximately 26 countries are transparent. Significant changes in the prices of existing shares are communicated to the customer with a ringtone. For starters, this stock trading software is perfect. The online purchase of a share is easy to perform with this software.

The Shareholder Standard program is not just software that can be used in the areas of stock exchange and trading. The custody account administration is guaranteed, as well as the stock market analyzes can help the customer. Chart analysis is the perfect tool for stock trading beginners and advanced. This software enables simplified trading activities.

A stock trading software test ensures accurate results

Well-known brokers were participants in this test. The highest score is 30.

Banks usually use their own developed software. Good trading platforms provide data for real price determination. ProRealTime was tested winner and is provided by broker IG. In another stock trading software test, Gopro took first place. Special features of this software:

- Gopro is available for free,
- the platform is extremely user-friendly,

Automatic stock exchange trading is guaranteed.

However, no corresponding app can be used for mobile use. For beginners and at the same time for professionals, this software is ideal. Prerequisite for use is an account with the broker GBE, the opening of the account can be done directly through the software. The software enables the opening of a demo account and a live account. The extremely well-designed platform allows the setting in four areas. The corresponding statistics inform the user about the status of the respective shares. Over 50 indicators and six chart types simplify stock trading. This software establishes a direct connection to the broker. The Trader Workstation has several advantages:

- Reliable order execution,
- 60 order types are available
- Scanners to monitor the market closely,
- Real-time courses in conjunction with the corresponding charts.
- Proposals for order execution at the lowest market price.

What speaks for a good stock trading software?

The recommended software must have some properties, such as:

Price fluctuations must be reliable and up-to-date communicated to the customer, the courses are the A and O of the stock trading.

News about relevant events related to the courses must be up to date. The so-called news ticker provides information on the current state of political and economic situations, which may influence the prices.

Reliable chart analysis is an important factor, but it adapts to the individual needs of the client.

The costs should always be kept low.

Obviously, finding the right broker is a priority, even before choosing the right software.

Broker software comparison

This comparison presents the optimal stock trading software and the perfect broker:

MetaTrader 4 is presented by brokers IG Markets and FXCM. The statements are actually made in milliseconds. The software is fast, easy and customer friendly. MetaTrader 4 is known worldwide and is used by most traders because this software can also be used on mobile devices.

Active Trader provides the bank Cortal Consors. This powerful software provides free real-time courses. Windows, Macintosh, Linux, and mobile devices enable flexible use. The additional chart module allows even more convenient use.

The GTS software is provided by broker OnVista Bank. Foreign exchange trading is handled with this special software. Additional modules provide even more functions.

Trading Station can be found at Broker FXCM. The charting tools are on the desktop. The free demo account will be filled with the virtual balance of 50,000 euros. The download is not necessary, the Internet connection is sufficient.

The software **Xtick** is very popular thanks to the real-time analysis. Over 80 indicators enable the professional compilation of own charts. After an eight-day trial, Xtick is no longer free to use.

Advantages of stock trading software

Different categories are clearly arranged and displayed, making transactions faster and more reliable. Serious price changes will be communicated to the trader in a timely manner. Stock sales are easier to execute. Special features of the different software:

- The software helps with relevant decisions,
- the variety of software is customer-friendly and easy to handle,
- the course information is reliable and presented promptly, in most cases in real time.
- The trading software is not always free. Regardless of the quality of the software and any costs, the trader should be satisfied that the product meets his personal requirements.

- The important thing is the charting tools. The prices of the shares can be presented in different time units. The presentation of the charting tools is different in each software, so often the decision depends on it. Who wants to load software on the computer will be satisfied with MetaTrader 4. The free stock trading demo account is helpful and indispensable for many professional traders. There are traders who may be the stock trading software of the broker, however, regardless of which MetaTrader 4 also use. Many functions are useful for stock trading with the MetaTrader 4 software. Each trader works on different assumptions, so MetaTrader 4 may not appeal to another trader. However, it is advantageous that there is a variety of stock trading software, so every customer can test and find his own software. The brokers usually provide their own trading software, but not every customer likes it. The software versions of the brokers often only allow the basic functions. The professional trader is of course not satisfied with these services and goes in search of a suitable stock trading software. MetaTrader and Ninja Traders are ideal for this purpose. AmiBroker includes the fastest analysis programs and focuses on the courses and price data.

Conclusion

It is noteworthy that some quality software can be used free of charge. Therefore, it is not surprising that traders are not just the stock trading software provided by the broker, but also use its own stock trading software. The software is designed to facilitate trading activities and is helpful in assisting necessary information related to stock trading with important decisions. Charts and analytics are also indispensable to the trader and are used with the software. Many brokers allow the use of MetaTrader software; For some customers, this software is enough. All important functions are enabled by the software; the easy operation is proverbial. It is known that the stock trader does not work without strategy; usually, he works out his own strategy. The demo account enables the trader to test the strategy. Most software are concise and are of great value to the stock trader. It is important to have a transparent presentation of the securities in the portfolio and price fluctuations. News that often influences stock prices is presented promptly to the client thanks to the stock trading software. The chart analysis offers probably every software.

WARREN BUFFETT: THE MOST SUCCESSFUL INVESTOR IN THE 20TH CENTURY

He is the man behind Berkshire Hathaway, with the most recent $ 262,350 most expensive stock in the world. He is the third richest person on the planet. He is called the "Oracle of Omaha" among investors. Warren Buffett, now 86 years old, has been shaping the investment world for decades. When Mr. Buffett speaks, everyone listens.

And yet Warren Buffett is a man who gets by without glamor and glamor. He lives in the same house that he bought in 1958 as a young man with his wife, looks like the friendly elderly gentleman next door and does not peddle his successes. That's why he is so admired. He seems like "one of us", not like some super-rich people who seem to live in another world, where law and decency are a problem for other people. Warren Buffet shows that each one of us is capable of being as successful as he is. That it is only him and not many others, however, has its reasons.

Goods buffet: "Businessman" from the age of six

If you read the life story of Warren Buffett, you have to smile involuntarily. For one thing, because you can imagine so much these kind elderly gentlemen starting to do their first "business" at the age of six. On the other hand, because there is an involuntary impression that it has to be someone like him, who not only achieves great success in the end but also knows how to preserve it. By the way, the life story of stock market legend André Kostolany (1906 - 1999) is similar.

Warren Buffett was born in 1930 as the second child of a broker. That may have been the basis that he realized from his earliest childhood that making money is not that hard. He started his business career at the age of six, buying six-packs of Coca-Cola for 25 cents and selling the bottles for five cents. Five cents of profit per six-pack - a return of 20 percent ... and then a dollar was worth even more than today. Later, he also sold used golf balls - all things that seem like everyone could get the idea. But somebody just has to be the first to go - and that's exactly what Warren Buffet is.

He also has a degree in economics from New York's Columbia University. And his studies have undoubtedly formed the foundation of the necessary theoretical knowledge for his career as an investor. But that Warren Buffet has been so much more successful than anyone else, based on something else:

The "superpowers" of Warren Buffett

Prudence, patience and the ability to acknowledge and learn from mistakes. These are the key three "superpowers" that distinguish Mr. Buffett from us. Right, actually we can all do that too. But Mr. Buffett could almost always. On the other hand, in the one more often, in the other less often, the emotions constantly spark in between. When sudden, extreme changes occur, the adrenaline rushes up and we fall into "fight-or-flight" syndrome:

The main thing is to do something! Escape or attack, no matter what, only immediately! On the stock market, the most expensive. Warren Buffett, on the other hand, kept the necessary calm for a decade at a time, even making a fortune out of mistakes. And his holding Berkshire Hathaway was the best example.

Buffett worked until 1956 for a short time after graduation as a securities analyst but then moved to operate an investment pool. This "buffet partnership" existed until 1969 and achieved on average over the years of its existence returns of almost 30 percent per year. This pool was dissolved in 1969. At that time, Buffett offered its investors to transfer their shares to the newly formed Berkshire Hathaway holding - at $ 43 per share.

The Berkshire Hathaway stock (ISIN: US0846701086) since 1990. Pay attention to the scaling on the left, it does not pay a dollar, but a thousand dollars each. Current Price $ 262,350!

Berkshire Hathaway: From big mistake to unique success story

Warren Buffett had already built up stakes in companies in his Buffet Partnership, which seemed lucrative to him. It was never about influence. He did not interfere with his investments because he was investing there because he was sure he knew what to do there. But at the textile company Berkshire Hathaway, he realized he had made a mistake.

Over time, he realized that the company would not prevail against increasing competition from the southern United States and Asia. Actually, he wanted to repel the stake. But after a break in the words of the then managing director, he took over Berkshire completely and began transforming the company into a holding company.

In the late sixties, Buffett took over insurance and a bank. For decades, the insurance and, above all, the reinsurance business was the holding company's biggest source of income, while the textile business was successively downsized and completely discontinued in the mid-eighties. Interesting: Berkshire Hathaway was not only never split as a stock, but it was also never paid a dividend. With the gains achieved, Buffett increased its investment portfolio.

The only concession to investors was the introduction of a "Baby Berkshire Share" in 1996 (ISIN: US0846707026). Since then, you can trade A-shares, the "Big Berkshire" in 1,500 B-shares, which then continue to exist and are also tradable on the stock market. However, the B share has 1 / 1,500 value of the A share, but only 1 / 10,000 voting rights.

In recent years, purchases of large blocks of shares from leading companies such as Apple, Coca Cola, the Washington Post, Munich Re or American Express have made headlines. But Berkshire Hathaway also has a large number of companies, some of which are well known. Berkshire Hathaway is one of Fruit of the Loom, Duracell, RC Wiley or Businesswire.

The principles of "Buffett investment"

Throughout the years, Buffett has remained reluctant to interfere in the affairs of his companies and holdings. While, according to data from February 2017, approximately 367,000 people are employees of the Berkshire Hathaway companies, the number of people working for Berkshire Hathaway is only 25, including Buffett. That's one of the key elements that makes Warren Buffet's success. He himself sums it up again and again:

Berkshire Hathaway invests only in companies whose products we can understand. In companies that also have a positive long-term perspective, based on high earning power, good, attractive products and a sufficiently long, successful history. We have to be able to trust corporate management. That means there must be competent and honest people. And the valuation of the company must be favorable.

Berkshire Hathaway and Dow Jones in direct performance comparison: Berkshire shareholders have doubled over the last decade.

That sounds simple. And that's it. You could also say: buy something good if it is cheap and keep your hands off investments that do not meet all these criteria.

Actually, we could all that too. But hardly anyone is able to so consistently stick to their own principles for so long. Again and again, the emotions come into play and throw sticks into our spokes. And in many of us, there is also a secretive player, who always demands his right. Warren Buffett, the nice billionaire next door, combines patience, intelligence, inventiveness, and reason in a degree that hardly anyone else succeeds. And because he has remained "one of us" precisely because of these qualities, he is rightly seen as a great role model and loved.

It's a good thing that Mr. Buffett lets investors participate in his abilities and that, since the "Baby Berkshire" exists, even those who do not have a quarter of a million left for a single stock can benefit from his abilities. Success proves him right, as highlighted in the chart above, which compares the performance of the Dow Jones and the Berkshire Hathaway. A stock over the past decade (right-hand scale). That's what Warren Buffet has to do to someone.

10 PRECAUTIONS TO TAKE BEFORE INVESTING IN A STOCK MARKET

To take advice, to invest the money that is not needed in the near future, to decide what percentage of losses it is willing to assume are some advice offered by experts to inexperienced people interested in playing on the stock market.

The stock market can be very attractive to obtain high returns with savings. However, it is a very complex scenario where you have to act in a reflexive way so as not to lose the investment, or to lose as little as possible.

Entities and financial managers encourage to move your money on the stock exchange not only to millionaires and experts but also to small savers since you can find values for all types of investors: large, modest, risky, conservative, interested in the short, medium or long term ... There is no lower limit when investing. Of course, all of them must comply with the same obligations. And it is that the size of the investment does not generate exceptions.

Revenue on the stock market is obtained through the purchase of shares of companies and their subsequent sale when their price rises (this gain is called goodwill). Likewise, with the profits that the companies distribute among their shareholders (dividends), the sale of rights in the capital increases and the shares received in a capital increase released.

Before entering the stock market it is necessary to know some of the requirements with which investors will find themselves. The purchase and sale of securities, the collection of dividends, custody of securities and capital increases involve the payment of commissions to financial intermediaries that must be contracted to operate on the stock market. The investor can not do it directly. Likewise, the obtained profits are taxed. For example, the capital gains generated by the sale of shares at a price higher than that acquired were considered capital gains and taxed as savings income. The dividends too.

1. **Advice and information**

Acting on the stock market can be profitable, but it is necessary to bear in mind that these are investments in equities. This means that you can earn as much as you can lose money. Therefore, the specialists, in addition to encouraging small savers to participate in it, point out some precautions that must be taken so that the experience is not unsatisfactory.

Advice

The previous step of a small novice investor without financial training should be to acquire basic knowledge of the stock market: more important concepts, operation, rights, and obligations.

Specialists consider it equally important to have advice when making an investment since stocks and other financial products need a technical analysis to assess whether they are appropriate for the objectives you want to achieve with the investment.

2. Invest in a thoughtful way

The stock market offers products for different investor profiles, this makes it easier to choose the most suitable for people willing to make risky bets or for more conservative investors. It is important to reflect and be clear about what you want to achieve with the investment and the deadline to achieve it. It is also essential to decide what percentage of losses you are willing to assume.

3. Invest money that is not needed

It is recommended to invest only the money that is safe is not going to be needed in the near future and whose loss does not represent a serious disruption to the investor's economy. First-time savers are advised to start with small, medium and long-term investments. This will allow them to learn about the operation of the bag and, later, you can risk something more if you are interested.

4. Be informed

Investors must constantly inform themselves about the investment made: collect data of the chosen company and follow its evolution, as well as their actions ... This knowledge can be obtained from the documentation sent by the contracted financial intermediary, as in the portals of the stock market and in the economic press.

5. The right choice

Short, medium or long term

Investing in the short term (less than a year) is very risky. You can get quick profits, but also losses. This option requires a great experience on the part of the investor. For novice savers, longer investment periods are recommended. Many experts believe that the medium term (between one and five years) is the most profitable.

6. Avoid speculative investments

These types of investments are very volatile. They are not the best option for small investors and even less for first-timers. Neither should action be acquired by being guided by rumors. The contrasting information is the best guide for buying shares and other financial products.

7. Do not buy falling values

It is not advisable to acquire values in full fall. It is better to let them touch bottom and buy when they begin to rise, although the price is more expensive.

8. Choose solvent companies

One should avoid investing in companies with a serious financial situation, according to the experts, who advise always selecting the solvents. Investors without experience are advised to start with shares of large companies since they can obtain more and better information to assess the suitability of purchase and make a subsequent follow-up.

9. Diversification

The danger of losing money on the stock market is reduced if the portfolio of securities is diversified if shares of different sectors or different sizes are acquired. The greater the diversification, the more distributed the risk will be.

10. Indirect investment

Those small savers who do not dare to play in the stock market have the possibility of doing it indirectly, through investment funds managed by entities and financial professionals.

KEY QUESTIONS TO LEARN TO INVEST IN THE STOCK MARKET

Currently, there are a variety of alternatives in which we can invest our capital but if what you want is to learn to invest in the stock market there are certain key questions that you must answer initially before entering this business.

These questions can be answered below so do not stop reading them.

Solve your doubts to learn how to invest

The following questions and answers that you will find here are key when starting to invest in the stock market:

❖ **What should you keep in mind when choosing to buy the shares of a company?** When you want to invest in securities you need to start looking for information about the company you want to invest in. You need to look for information about the current financial situation but you should also know about the process of developing it. In this way and to learn how to invest in the stock market it is necessary that you learn to study and review the financial data of the companies. Only in this way can you decide considering timely and real data.

❖ **But the study of the financial information of the company is not the only thing you have to consider to choose to buy certain shares.** Actually, it is very important that you also review the evolution of the quotation that the company has presented on the stock exchange. Verify the profitability and dividends of the shares clearly taking into account your expectations and the level of risk you are willing to assume.

❖ **What are brokers?** Many people when looking to learn how to invest in the stock market encounter this word. For it must be clear that the broker is presented as an intermediary whose objective is to make the purchase and sale of securities in this market. They are also known as commission companies, which have extensive experience in this market. Brokers offer their services to investors who wish to enter this market and do so through a commission contract. In doing so, they will represent their clients and carry out the respective negotiations for the purchase and sale of securities.

- **The broker is an experienced professional who can advise and advise but the final decision of the negotiations must always be made by the investor.**

   It is also necessary to clarify that these professionals can operate within a bank or also as a natural person. The important thing when choosing a broker to hire is that it is regulated by government financial institutions in the country as well as by the market self-regulator.

- **Commissions to be paid, what are they?** Before investing in the stock market, you must know that if you hire a broker, it is necessary to consider paying certain fees. These intermediaries handle different rates and it is that each one of them has the freedom to establish the value. Now and as the broker has the freedom to establish the value by the commission as investors, you also have the freedom to choose this broker.

- **Now and if the rates change from one intermediary to another what should be known are the names of those commissions that are major.** The most common is the purchase and sale, then maintenance, also handled the collection of dividends as well as capital increases. If you decide to change broker you must make the payment for change if you have decided to transfer the shares to another intermediary.

- ❖ **How much capital is needed to start investing?** Generally, people believe that for this business to be profitable it requires a lot of money to invest. Actually, the possibilities in this market are very broad and they adapt to several budgets. For example, some products are presented at really low prices, about 50 dollars, and they can be accessed through collective investment funds.

Finally, when learning to invest in the stock market, you must be very clear that each investment alternative presents a risk profile. This varies considerably depending on the product chosen and therefore before investing it is necessary to study the options well and choose the one that best suits your expectations and needs.

WHICH METHOD IS BETTER TO MAKE MONEY IN THE STOCK MARKET?

If you ask me which method is best to make money in the stock market, long-term investing or "trading" would not be an easy question to answer.

My personal opinion is that you should try different ways to invest - long and short term, and use focus on the ones you feel most comfortable with (day trading, options, futures, and currencies) - until you find the one that works for you. To do this, documéntate very well, make a thorough study of each of the ways to invest before risking your money.

Always remember that it is your money and no one but you affects both your loss and the profits.

Then I explain what I consider are the advantages and disadvantages of investing and doing "trading"

TO INVEST

Advantage:

- From a statistical point of view, in the long term, the chances of success are greater than those of a trader
- The odds of having consistent returns year after year are higher than those of a "trader"
- It takes less time
- Psychologically it is less stressful than doing "trading"
- Less expensive than trading since the number of transactions is lower

Disadvantages:

- If the investment goes well, the returns for generating it are lower than those for the short term
- You are likely to lose interest due to the fact that you are not involved in daily transactions, so you can neglect the investment and reduce the chances of making the investment grow and, in many cases, risk losing money

TRADING

Advantage:

- If you succeed as a "trader", the profits are usually much higher than those of an investor
- You can use many more tools to make money in the short term more effectively. For example, stop orders, short-selling, Trailing orders, etc ...
- The successful trade can make money when the stock rises and also when the stock falls, while the investor usually depends on the appreciation of the stock to grow its portfolio.

Disadvantages:

- Costs are high due to a large number of transactions that are made daily.
- Much more time is required.
- There is no doubt that it is a much more stressful way of making money. It is recommended only to people with "steel temperament", able to control the tensions produced by the strong and frequent fluctuations of the market.

I do not recommend one technique more than the other. What I do suggest is that you analyze what type of investment goes with your personality, your needs, the time you can spend, knowledge of the different tools and your capacity and tolerance against risk. We found more successful people as an investor than as a "trader". To become a successful trader, it requires, in addition to time and discipline, very specific psychological conditions that allow managing the tensions that the activity produces. As an investor, it is less complicated, you choose a group of mutual funds or fundamentally stable shares and you only have to wait for the return on investment, a return that is generally higher than what most "traders" would have in 10 years. Finally, I can recommend you, if you have the time,

HOW TO ACHIEVE CONSISTENCY IN TRADING? MAIN BASIC RULES TO FOLLOW

Every professional trader who values himself will agree with the following statement: the consistency in trading is the ultimate goal of any trader who wants to dedicate himself to this. The consistency in trading is closely linked to stability, consolidation, duration concept. The aim is to obtain a continuous and constant income, the key to success being the confidence we have in ourselves.

Consistency in trading equals perseverance, patience and confidence.

The emotional state of the trader is vital when trading. The psychology of trading or psycho trading is an area of study of utmost importance for those who intend to live from trading since our internal limits can lead to failure if we do not overcome them. Operating in an optimal mental state is necessary to achieve success and that means knowing oneself to recognize the internal limitations that we have and learn to overcome them.

Thus, psycho trading is one of the facets that should not be neglected and should be worked on, just as analytical studies are used to predict the behavior of the market because consistency is not something that is achieved magically and instantaneously. In fact, to achieve consistency we must eliminate the mistakes we make (and I do not mean the losing operations derived from the strategy or system itself) but those we commit by not knowing ourselves.

The professional trader reaches it able to overcome the hard times that occur, as in all work, learning every day; ending by drawing his own strategy to follow.

The consistency in trading lies in achieving success in a prolonged manner, it is not momentary and transient. For this reason, many point to consistency as the secret of success.

What to do to achieve consistency in trading?

At this point, it is normal that doubts arise about which actions are the most suitable to achieve consistency in trading.

If you are looking to become a professional and consistent trader, you must take certain actions with the aim of working on your confidence and patience in trading.

1.- First of all, it is essential that you have training and be aware of the financial field from beginning to end. This background will be vital to overcome the initial fears to launch on the market. (If you are looking for training you can access my professional online trading course)

2.- Training and learning take time. Take time to improve your analytical skills and explore techniques and tools to operate. Learning to read and interpret the market is not a matter of a couple of hours.

3.- Build your own trading system. Each system is personal and what works for another does not have to work for you. These systems, according to the psycho trading, must adapt to your needs and, above all, to your personality. When you have it defined, work on its daily improvement and apply it with patience.

4.- Do not pressure yourself to get a stipulated amount per day. Focus on applying your system and improving your technique, this is the principle.

5.- We make the mistake of focusing everything on the money, on the results of the operations, but the reality is that the benefits come after doing your trading well, not before, remember that the one that grows your portfolio depends on how you do all the steps correctly and as a result you will have the expected benefits.

6. Initially, try to trade in a specific market easily predictable and with which you are familiar, to gain skill and work confidence.

7.- Manage the risk in a consistent manner. Calculate the capital that you are willing to lose by operation and do not get out of this way.

8.- It is important that you work on accepting losses because not everything is profit. You have to be aware that in trading sometimes you win and sometimes you lose, it is impossible to have a 100% success rate; this is a long distance race in which you should not stop running. Therefore, the psychology of trading emphasizes preparing mentally and emotionally to operate in the markets. If you do not do it, the losses will end up taking you out of the market.

9.- The moment you start to obtain, on a regular basis, benefits, try to keep them stable for a period of time, do not get blind with wanting to earn more, keep your daily goals.

10.- Dominate your emotions and build structured habits, I mean not to lose sight of your trading plan, and I'll tell you more, build a work plan in parallel, as if you were doing the administration of a company, profit calculator and expenses.

All this will make you never lose perspective of where you are, not entering the market in a crazy way and taking totally unnecessary risks, if you can do it right, why do it wrong. It will also help you to work with more decision and more concentration, and this will eventually turn into favorable results.

Follow this list of actions to work on consistency in trading.

Remember that this is not done by doing it, the goal is to internalize the concepts and believe in you, with the goal of becoming consistent. In this way, you will achieve the environment in which a professional trader breathes, an environment of motivation and calm in a sector that is accelerated.

It is, ultimately, to achieve the desired goal, which we all want to achieve, to achieve our own consistency.

5 FINANCIAL TOOLS ESSENTIAL FOR TRADERS AND INVESTORS

Do not be fooled to trade or invest in the stock market, you need a minimum of tools. Few of these tools are really necessary. It is also very easy and tempting to surround yourself with a panoply of tools and equipment believing that the more we have, and the more we look pro! Or even, the more one surrounds oneself with an arsenal of war and the more one will succeed. Just see the picture below to be sure.

There is also a plethora of companies that are ready to sell you anything and everything in this juicy industry. For an industry that can earn money is inherently an extremely profitable industry.

In the stock market, you need to look for simple and effective solutions for several reasons:

The more complicated you are, the more difficult it is later to really understand what is happening, or even who influences what?

The more parameters, systems or tools you have to take into account, the more difficult it is to manage them effectively, measure them, test them, improve them and start again.

And all these elements to take into account are also totally valid to choose your own tools on the stock market.

So you need to limit yourself to the bare minimum. Here, I will limit myself to the following 5 tools that I consider indispensable for traders and investors to start well.

We will now see what they are and why they are indispensable.

Tool 1: A computer with internet access

For the computer, a PC running Windows or Linux or a Mac is perfect. And that's good, almost everyone has one at home. And the technical features are no longer important nowadays. ALL recent machines (less than 2 years old) are quite powerful enough to do the trick!

I will not dwell on the reasons why we need a computer, they are rather obvious: all the other tools we will see are without exception computer tools. We live in the 21st century, no need to draw a picture. No more phone calls to the broker and all the information on paper

I personally have an iMac 27 "(desktop) and a MacBook 11" (laptop) for various reasons.

I do not do anything on the MacBook about the stock market and my trading. The resolution is a little weak for viewing multiple data, graphs and technical indicators at the same time.

I use it anyway from time to time, it's when I'm traveling. There, I do not really have other solutions and it's super convenient. On vacation, I avoid the maximum and I invite you to do the same, otherwise, it's more holidays. So on the move, it's ok but it's not nearly as comfortable as at home. It's convenient too if I have a problem with the iMac.

The bulk of the work for the stock market is done on the iMac: trading with the broker, track quotes, manage the portfolio and maintain the trading log. You do not need a second big screen if you already have a big one. If your main screen is small enough, then why not a second screen ...

For internet access, any ADSL connection will do the trick. Even if huge investments are currently being made between the US and Europe to gain a few microseconds (see high-frequency trading), I can tell you without being too wrong that you are like me, you have no need

For my part, I have fiber optics at home in Mauritius with 100 Mbps and it degrades seriously! It's even more than I had in London when I left, but the flows have risen in London since!

Tool 2: An Online Broker

There are now many ways to make money on the stock market without having to open an account with a conventional broker, that is to say from your bank. I hope this is not your case, otherwise, you can start looking for alternatives right away to have a lot better with other online brokers.

For information, a broker is called a " stockbroker " in English or simply " broker ". You will see quite often this English word used on the net rather than the word " stockbroker ". Depending on which country you live in, you can access currencies, live stocks, CFDs, options, futures, funds, etc. It has never been easier and easier to buy and sell stock market products in the financial markets.

The best thing about getting started is to buy and resell live through an online broker and not a conventional broker (usually your bank) for the following reasons:

- The tools are usually simpler to discover and understand.
- The costs are much lower
- Accessible products are much more numerous
- Service is faster, more convenient and easier

Your online broker allows you to trade your products on the stock market. It is he who will then automatically execute the order for you in the markets. Your transaction is usually registered in your account and you can access it later to view different information such as the date of the transaction, the quantity involved in the transaction, the price at the time of the transaction, the cost price, performance, etc.

Brokers in France will offer you the 3 tax envelopes to invest in the stock market. They represent the different types of accounts that you can use to perform these trading operations. Some other brokers in Europe targeting the French clientele will also offer you these tax envelopes or types of stock market account. For brokers outside Europe, they will only offer securities accounts.

Depending on the chosen tax envelope and the selected broker, you will have access to different stock exchanges or markets such as Euronext, the New York Stock Exchange (NYSE), the London Stock Exchange (LSE), the Nasdaq, etc.

The online broker is, therefore, your indispensable intermediary between you and the stock markets.

Tool 3: Access to stock quotes and market info

Now that you have an account open to a stockbroker to buy and sell securities, you usually have to use other sites or tools to access stock quotes and market info.

Why? ... Some of this information is available with your broker but they are often VERY basic and not enough to find real nuggets.

Here are the stock information and features you need most :

The graphics of an action or a particular industry, spanning the course, volumes and proposing indicators technical for additional information

Of screeners for filtering titles (such as ranking of increases and decreases over time) or replicants titles particular criteria

News related to your securities or those of interest such as the times when companies are in stock earnings reports (past and present)

The dividend that will be or have been paid by a company which you own titles

The fundamental or financial information on a company or sector

A backtest tool for testing simulations and strategies on historical prices

The solution I recommend for actions: ProRealTime - Software (PRT)!

Tool 4: A tool to manage your stock market portfolio

A tool to manage your stock market portfolio is mainly used to easily track your investments and their performance.

The simplest method (aside from the paper and the pen) is to use a spreadsheet like with Excel, Apple Numbers, Google Spreadsheets or with OpenOffice. With a spreadsheet you can:

Save your inputs, outputs, trade sizes, commissions, and offsets

Take evaluation notes of your trades and sources of ideas for other trades

Access your transaction history

Access operations on your portfolio such as contributions, withdrawals, custody fees, etc.

Access transactions on your transactions such as dividends, awards, subscription rights, etc.

Access graphs like those mentioned in the previous section but also your own gains and losses

Access the real valuation of your portfolio and have a summary

If your stock management tool is integrated with a data feed or your broker, it's even better!

Personally, I use a spreadsheet in Apple's Numbers format and I combine that with the reports provided by my broker.

Tool 5: A trading log

A trading journal may seem optional, but it is, in fact, an ESSENTIAL tool for your success on the stock market.

A trading diary is an illustrated record of all your trades. It documents your inputs and outputs and if possible with graphics to visualize these levels using arrows and lines. It should also include your own comments on the different aspects of your trades, such as your emotions when you opened and closed a position.

You must update your trading journal regularly after each entry and exit. Then, it is good to do a detailed analysis of a posteriori of all your notes and operations. Do it at least once a month or quarter to try to understand your mistakes, your successes, your mistakes or successes repeatedly. The goal is to optimize your system and your approach.

Keeping a trading journal is the most important tool to become a good trader or investor!

Technically this trading log can be combined with other tools that we just saw before. For example, you can have all this information in your tool to manage your stock portfolio, so a spreadsheet. It can also be combined with your stock market access solution as with PRT.

The tools that I deliberately omitted

Here are some tools that I decided to deliberately omit because I do not consider them important or essential in the stock market, or at least to start:

- **Commercialized automatic or semiautomatic trading systems:** these are black boxes where we do not really understand what is happening. It's pretty dangerous with your own money!

- **Miracle methods:** none works, do not hide your face. What seems too good to be true is often so. Everyone would be rich easily ... and that's far from reality. There are good methods and training on the market, but none is "miraculous"!

- **Gadgets (tablet, smartphone, dozens of screens, etc ..):** And yet I am a "nerd/geek" by nature as likes to remind me my English wife But to make the stock market on such tools is a joke. It's good to play casino or show off. But to really win the stock market, you can forget. And you are likely to fall into the trap of overtrading being little more concentrated!

We have just seen the 5 essential tools for traders and investors with explanations to better understand what they are and why they are essential.

There is a sixth tool; it is not really one, but it is just as essential if not more, it is training. Be equipped with good training and an experienced person all the time at your side to accompany you on the stock market. Do not stay alone.

CONCLUSION: MAKE TRADING WORTH YOUR TIME

That's all you need to know in the field. While none of these techniques provide, a guarantee of success if used by itself, a combination of the above techniques can provide the day trader an edge if he/she is quick. However, while the profits may come quickly with day trading, one must be aware that the losses can come just as fast, and in most cases even faster with more devastating results. If you are planning on becoming a day trader, do as much research and practice before you put down any of your own money!

The goal with your quiet time is to think or reflect what is going on with your trading.

Evaluate your situation outside of the cycle of fine-tuning your trading method can often lead you to a potential new approach to your trading business. There may be ways to improve your decision-making process on how you engage the market. There are also changes to the market behavior due to issues like policy changes and structural changes which require your awareness so that you are well prepared for their potential impacts.

If you do not sit down and think about these issues, you will be stuck within your existing approach and decline yourself the performance boost you could have.

From this perspective, trading is no different from any other businesses - it needs you to put in your best efforts to grow it bigger. Work smarter, not harder.

APPRECIATION

We sincerely appreciate your purchase of our e-Book that reveals useful information about everything you need to know about Stock Market Investing and Trading. We hope you love it!

Thanks!

Michael Stevenson.

www.ingramcontent.com/pod-product-compliance
Lightning Source LLC
Chambersburg PA
CBHW072213170526
45158CB00002BA/572